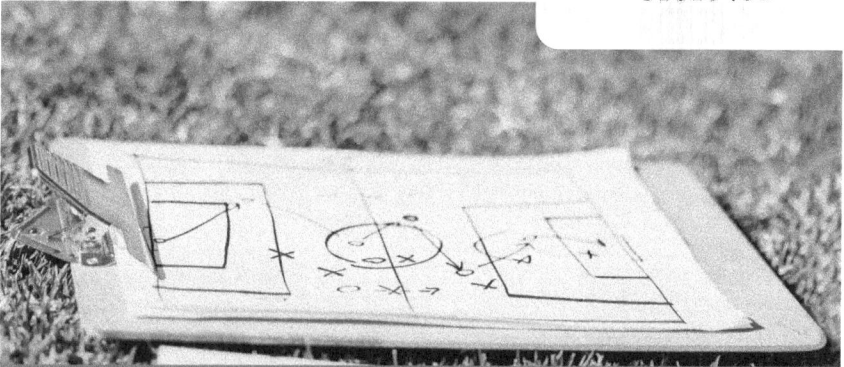

THE HOME SELLER'S PLAYBOOK

A Comprehensive Guide to Successfully Selling Your Home

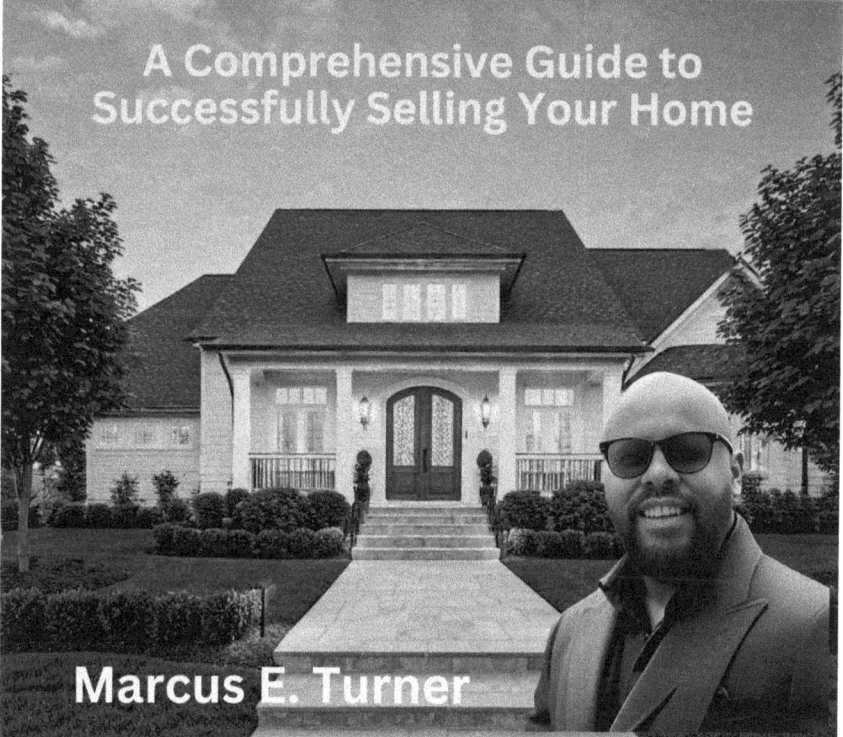

Marcus E. Turner

THE HOME SELLER'S PLAYBOOK

PLAYBOOK

A Comprehensive Guide to Successfully Selling Your Home

Marcus E. Turner

The Home Seller's Playbook
A Comprehensive Guide to Successfully Selling Your Home

Published by Zarephath Press (ISBN 978-0-9799414-3-6)

Dedicated to my late father,
Robert L. Turner

Served over 50 Years as
Principal and Owner of:

Robert L. Turner LTD
General Contractor
Builder/Developer
Portsmouth, VA

"I truly appreciate your dedication and the path you've created for me.
Your hard work has inspired me, and
I am grateful for the opportunity to follow in your footsteps."

TABLE OF CONTENTS

TABLE OF FIGURES

Setting the Stage for a Successful Sale

Preface

Selling your home represents more than a mere financial exchange; it signifies a pivotal transition that frequently heralds the start of a new phase in your life. Whether you're relocating, upgrading, downsizing, or pursuing a long-awaited dream, the process of selling your property can be both exciting and daunting. **This book is here to guide you, offering expert insights, practical advice, and proven strategies to help you navigate this journey with confidence and success.**

But why should you choose me to list and sell your home? The answer is simple: I'm not just a real estate professional; **I'm your partner in achieving the best possible outcome for one of the most important decisions of your life.** Let me show you why entrusting me with the sale of your home is a decision you won't regret.

A GLOBAL NETWORK AT YOUR SERVICE

In today's interconnected world, real estate transactions often transcend borders. Whether you're relocating to a new city, moving across the country, or even venturing internationally, my extensive network of Realtors® ensures that **I can assist you with all your real estate needs—no matter where you are.**

As an international real estate consultant, I've cultivated relationships with trusted professionals across all states and countries. This allows me to easily assign and refer agents who are perfectly suited to assist you, regardless of your location. With certifications as a **Relocation Specialist, Military Relocation Professional, Senior Real Estate Specialist, Seller Representative Specialist,**

Pricing Strategy Advisor, and **Accredited Buyer Representative**, I'm uniquely equipped to guide you through every aspect of the buying or selling process with expertise and care.

"Marcus helped us get through the home buying process and overcome any challenges that came with VA loan appraisal and inspection. He communicated with multiple parties to ensure everyone is on the same page. Marcus provided clear answers to any questions or concerns we might have had. If you ever need a realtor, know that Marcus is a reliable source!"

UNDERSTANDING THE REAL ESTATE MARKET

The real estate market can feel like a puzzle, with its constant shifts and unpredictable trends. What's the right price for your home? When is the best time to sell? How do you attract serious buyers who will appreciate the unique value of your property? These are the questions that every seller grapples with—and the answers can make all the difference.

Here's where my expertise comes into play. **With years of experience navigating local and international markets, I bring a deep understanding of the dynamics that drive successful sales.** From analyzing market trends to assessing your property's unique selling points, I craft a customized strategy tailored to your goals.

As one client shared:

"Marcus is a very passionate and dedicated realtor. His many years of experience show as he helped navigate and negotiate my spouse and me to successfully close on our home."

To further ensure your success, I guarantee a comprehensive market analysis and pricing strategy within 48 hours of our listing appointment. This gives you the confidence of knowing your home is positioned perfectly in the current market.

First impressions matter—especially in real estate. Buyers decide within seconds whether a property feels like "home," which means your listing needs to shine from the very beginning.

This is why I go beyond the basics. I don't just help you clean and declutter; I provide expert advice on staging your home to highlight its best features. From professional photography that captures your property in its best light to compelling descriptions that tell its story, every detail is designed to create a powerful emotional connection with potential buyers.

Another client noted:

"Marcus demonstrates exceptional client service by always going above and beyond and thinking ahead. His caring approach and in-depth industry knowledge are invaluable assets. He excels at strategic decision-making, ensuring the best possible outcomes for his clients."

MARKETING THAT MOVES THE NEEDLE

In today's competitive market, simply putting up a "For Sale" sign is not enough. To attract the right buyers, your home needs visibility across multiple channels. That's where my comprehensive marketing approach comes in.

Your property will be showcased on all major online platforms, reaching a wide audience of motivated buyers. **I'll also leverage my network of local agents, real estate professionals, and past clients to create buzz and drive interest.** By combining traditional marketing methods with innovative digital strategies, I ensure that your home gets the attention it deserves.

NEGOTIATION: GETTING THE BEST DEAL

When offers start rolling in, the stakes are high. This is the moment when experience and skill make all the difference. **As your agent, I'm committed to protecting your interests and maximizing your return.**

"Tough negotiator. I'd rather him in my corner than with my opponent. It was an estate sale, which can be long and arduous, but we bobbed and weaved until close and got it done. Thanks for putting in the work."

Negotiation isn't just about getting the highest price—it's about securing terms that align with your goals. Whether it's timing, contingencies, or other factors, I'll guide you through the process with clarity and confidence. My goal is to ensure that every detail is in your favor, so you can move forward with peace of mind.

Why Choose Me?

There's no shortage of real estate agents, so why should you work with me? Because I bring more than just expertise—I bring a personal commitment to your success.

Proven Results: My track record speaks for itself. With a history of successful transactions and satisfied clients, I know what it takes to sell homes quickly and at top dollar.

Local Knowledge: As someone deeply familiar with the area, I understand what buyers are looking for and how to position your property to stand out.

Tailored Approach: No two homes—or sellers—are the same. I take the time to understand your unique needs and goals, crafting a personalized plan that aligns with your vision.

Unwavering Support: Selling a home can be stressful, but you don't have to do it alone. I'm here to answer your questions, address your concerns, and provide guidance every step of the way.

As one client remarked:

"Wow! What an amazing job Marcus did on the transaction we had together. I'm amazed at how fast he responded and was able to help guide and assist me through the process. He was very knowledgeable about questions regarding the contract and offer. Highly recommended to anybody needing an agent in the DMV."

Taking the First Step

If you're ready to sell your home, the journey begins with a single step: reaching out. Together, we'll assess your property, discuss your goals, and create a roadmap for success.

"Marcus helped us get through the home buying process and overcome any challenges that came with VA loan appraisal and inspection. He communicated with multiple parties to ensure everyone is on the same page. Marcus provided clear answers to any questions or concerns we might have had. If you ever need a realtor, know that Marcus is a reliable source!"

Don't wait for the perfect moment—make it happen. Contact me today, and let's start turning your real estate dreams into reality.

With me by your side, you'll have the confidence of knowing that every decision is guided by expertise, integrity, and a genuine commitment to your success. So let's make this journey a rewarding one—together.

Your Success Story Starts Here

This book is your guide, but it's also an invitation—to take control of your selling journey, to maximize the value of your home, and to achieve the results you deserve. And with my help, you'll not only meet your goals—you'll exceed them. **Let's get started.**

Welcome to the Selling Journey

Chapter One

Selling a home is an exciting and transformative process, often marking the start of a new chapter in life. Whether it's the first time you're putting your home on the market or you're a seasoned seller, this journey is both a practical undertaking and an emotional milestone. In this chapter, we'll explore the key aspects of selling a home, including what to expect, how to navigate the emotional and practical sides, and an overview of the steps involved—from your first considerations to closing day.

THE PROCESS OF SELLING A HOME

Selling a home involves more than just putting a "For Sale" sign in the yard; it's a multi-step process that requires careful planning, decision-making, and teamwork with real estate professionals. Understanding the journey ahead can empower you to make informed choices and achieve your selling goals.

The first step is evaluating your home's market value. This involves analyzing comparable sales in your area, current market conditions, and unique features of your property. Partnering with a Realtor® at this stage can provide valuable insights, as they bring local expertise and access to market data.

Next, you'll prepare your home for the market. This can include cleaning, decluttering, staging, and addressing any necessary repairs or upgrades. A well-presented home creates a strong first impression and can lead to faster sales and better offers.

Once your home is listed, marketing becomes key. Your agent will showcase your property through high-quality photos, virtual tours, and multiple listing platforms, reaching a wide audience of potential buyers. Showings and open houses follow, allowing prospective buyers to experience your home firsthand.

When offers come in, the negotiation process begins. Your agent will help you review offers, counter when needed, and work toward terms that align with your goals. After accepting an offer, you'll move into the escrow phase, where inspections, appraisals, and financing approvals take place.

Finally, the closing day arrives—signaling the official transfer of ownership. At this stage, all paperwork is completed, funds are exchanged, and keys are handed over to the new owner.

WHAT YOU CAN EXPECT

Selling a home is a journey with highs and lows, but preparation is your best ally. Homeowners can expect a process that requires patience, adaptability, and decision-making, often in a dynamic and fast-moving market.

One thing to anticipate is the importance of timing. Market conditions can heavily influence your selling experience. In a seller's market, where demand exceeds supply, you might receive multiple offers quickly. Conversely, in a buyer's market, it may take longer to attract interest. Collab-orating with your Realtor® to assess market trends can help set realistic expectations.

Homeowners should also expect feedback and adjustments along the way. Buyers may provide comments during showings or request repairs after inspections. While it's natural to feel attached to your home, being open to constructive feedback can enhance your chances of a successful sale.

Financial considerations are another key aspect of what to expect. Beyond the sale price, there are closing costs, agent commissions, and potential repair expenses to account for. Having a clear picture of these costs early on can help you budget and plan effectively.

Lastly, sellers can expect a range of emotions. Selling a home can bring excitement about the future, but it may also stir nostalgia and stress, especially if there are tight timelines or unexpected hurdles. Understanding that these feelings are normal can help you navigate the journey with resilience and clarity.

Selling a home is as much an emotional experience as it is a practical one. It's often more than just a transaction—it's the closing of one chapter and the beginning of another.

The Emotional Side

Homes hold memories, from milestone celebrations to quiet everyday moments. Saying goodbye to a space that has been a part of your life can bring mixed emotions. It's important to allow yourself time to process these feelings. Share your thoughts with friends or family, and focus on the opportunities that your next home will bring.

For some, the selling journey can feel overwhelming. The process of decluttering, staging, and preparing for showings may seem daunting. Breaking these tasks into smaller, manageable steps can make them feel less overwhelming.

If children are involved, they may have their own emotional responses to leaving a home they've grown up in. Open communication and involving them in the process—such as packing or choosing features for the new home—can ease the transition.

The Practical Side

On the practical front, selling a home involves strategic planning and execution. It's important to approach the process with a business mindset, focusing on decisions that will maximize your home's market appeal and financial return.

For example, depersonalizing the space by removing family photos and personalized décor can help buyers envision themselves in the home.

Small updates, like a fresh coat of paint or updated fixtures, can also make a big difference in how the home is perceived.

Organization is key during this process. From tracking appointments for showings to managing paperwork for inspections, staying organized can save time and reduce stress. Many homeowners find it helpful to create a timeline or checklist to ensure no detail is overlooked.

Balancing the emotional and practical aspects of selling requires flexibility and self-care. Taking time for yourself, celebrating milestones along the way, and seeking support from loved ones and professionals can help you navigate this complex but rewarding journey.

Steps Involved: From Initial Considerations to Closing Day

Understanding the steps involved in selling a home provides clarity and confidence as you move forward. Here's a high-level overview of the journey:

Step 1: Assess Your Situation
Begin by evaluating your reasons for selling and your goals. Are you relocating, downsizing, or upgrading? Your motivations will shape your priorities during the sale.

Assess your home's current market value, and consider consulting a real estate agent for a comparative market analysis (CMA). This step will give you insight into your home's potential price range.

Step 2: Prepare Your Home
Preparation is crucial for making a strong impression on buyers. Clean and declutter every room, removing personal items and excess belongings. Consider hiring a professional stager to showcase your home's best features.

Address any maintenance issues, such as leaky faucets, peeling paint, or broken fixtures. These small investments can go a long way in creating a polished presentation.

Step 3: Set the Right Price

Pricing your home competitively is essential. Overpricing may deter buyers, while underpricing could leave money on the table. Work with your agent to determine a price based on market conditions, comparable sales, and your home's unique attributes.

Step 4: Market Your Home

Your agent will create a marketing plan to attract potential buyers. This typically includes professional photography, virtual tours, online listings, and open houses. Highlighting your home's unique selling points, such as location, upgrades, or special features, can set it apart.

Step 5: Show Your Home

During showings and open houses, keep your home clean and inviting. Consider leaving during these events to give buyers space to envision themselves living there. Your agent will gather feedback from buyers to refine the marketing strategy if needed.

Step 6: Review and Negotiate Offers

When offers come in, your agent will present them to you, highlighting key terms such as price, contingencies, and closing timelines. Be prepared to negotiate to achieve the best possible terms.

Step 7: Navigate Inspections and Appraisals

Once an offer is accepted, the buyer may conduct inspections and the lender will arrange for an appraisal. Addressing repair requests and ensuring your home appraises for the agreed price are critical steps to keep the deal on track.

Step 8: Close the Sale

On closing day, all necessary documents are signed, funds are transferred, and the property ownership officially changes hands. Celebrate this milestone as you hand over the keys and begin your next chapter.

CONCLUSION

Selling a home is a journey that combines preparation, collaboration, and adaptability. By understanding the process, setting realistic expectations, and addressing both the emotional and practical aspects, you can navigate the selling experience with confidence. Welcome to the selling journey—here's to a successful and rewarding transition!

HOME SELLING JOURNEY

1 Assess Your Situation

2 Prepare Your Home

3 Set the Right Price

4 Market Your Home

5 Show Your Home

6 Review and Negotiate Offers

7 Navigate Inspections and Appraisals

8 Close the Sale

Figure 1

Deciding to Sell: Is It the Right Time?

Chapter Two

For many homeowners, deciding to sell their property is one of the most significant financial and personal decisions they will make. It's a decision influenced by a combination of market trends, personal circumstances, and long-term financial goals. With so many factors at play, how can you determine if now is the right time to sell? This chapter will help you evaluate whether selling your home is a smart decision, taking into account market trends, personal motivations, and financial considerations.

UNDERSTANDING MARKET TRENDS

Market conditions play a pivotal role in deciding whether to sell your home. By analyzing current trends, you can gauge the potential profitability and feasibility of listing your property. Here are key factors to consider:

Local Real Estate Market Conditions

Every housing market is different. Some areas may be experiencing a seller's market—where demand exceeds supply—resulting in higher prices and faster sales. In contrast, a buyer's market gives potential purchasers the upper hand, often leading to lower home prices and longer selling times. Researching local trends is essential.

– **Home Prices:** Are prices rising or stabilizing in your area? Increasing home values can signal a good time to sell, as you'll likely achieve a higher return on your investment.

– **Days on Market (DOM):** A lower DOM suggests strong demand, meaning homes are selling quickly.

– **Inventory Levels:** If there are fewer homes for sale relative to the number of buyers, it's often a favorable time for sellers.

Interest Rates

Mortgage interest rates directly affect buyers' purchasing power. When rates are low, buyers can afford higher-priced homes, which can drive demand. Conversely, rising interest rates might reduce the pool of qualified buyers, potentially softening prices.

Seasonal Trends

Historically, spring and early summer are peak times for home sales, with more buyers actively searching. However, selling during off-peak seasons like winter may have advantages, such as less competition from other sellers.

Economic Indicators

Economic health—such as job growth, consumer confidence, and inflation—can influence the housing market. Positive indicators often lead to robust demand, while economic uncertainty may dampen buyer enthusiasm.

Evaluating Personal Motivations

Market conditions aside, your reasons for selling are equally critical. Understanding your personal motivations can clarify whether now is the right time.

Lifestyle Changes

Life is dynamic, and your living situation should align with your current needs. Consider the following scenarios:

Growing Family: If your family is expanding, you might need more space. Selling your current home to upgrade to a larger one could be a practical solution.

Empty Nest: When children move out, downsizing can save money and reduce maintenance burdens.

Relocation: A new job, desire for better schools, or a move to be closer to family may necessitate selling.

Retirement: Selling a large or expensive-to-maintain home to move to a more manageable property often aligns with retirement goals.

Emotional Readiness

Selling a home is not just a financial decision—it's an emotional one. If you've built strong memories or attachments, parting ways can be difficult. Ask yourself if you're emotionally prepared to let go of your property and embrace a new chapter.

Timing Flexibility

If you don't have to sell immediately, you have the advantage of choosing a more strategic time. However, if your circumstances require an urgent sale, such as financial constraints or job relocation, you may need to prioritize speed over optimal market timing.

FINANCIAL CONSIDERATIONS

Selling a home involves both potential gains and costs. Assessing your financial readiness is crucial in determining if now is the right time to sell.

Current Home Equity

Equity—the difference between your home's market value and the amount you owe on your mortgage—is a key factor. High equity often translates to more financial flexibility when selling. To calculate your equity:

Home Equity = Current Market Value − Remaining Mortgage Balance

If your equity is low or negative (known as being "underwater"), selling may not be financially viable unless market conditions are exceptionally favorable.

Selling Costs

Selling a home isn't free. Prepare for expenses such as:

Real Estate Agent Listing Commissions: The price is consistently open to negotiation. Typically, a real estate agent will present a selection of services for clients to select from.

Closing Costs: Transfer taxes, attorney fees, and other administrative expenses.

Repairs and Staging: Enhancing your home's appeal may require minor repairs, landscaping, or professional staging.

Seller Concessions: Financial incentives that a seller offers to a buyer and or buyer broker to help make the purchase of a home more affordable and marketable.

Moving Costs: The cost of relocating your belongings to a new home.

Mortgage Payoff and Prepayment Penalties

Review your mortgage agreement for any penalties associated with early payoff. Ensure the proceeds from the sale will cover the mortgage balance and associated costs.

Future Housing Plans

Consider your next steps after selling:

Buying Another Home: Is it a good time to buy, or will you face inflated prices and stiff competition in your desired area?

Renting: If you're not ready to buy again, evaluate rental market conditions and availability.

Tax Implications

Selling a home may have tax consequences, particularly if your profit exceeds the federal capital gains tax exclusion limits ($250,000 for single filers, $500,000 for married couples). Consult a tax professional to l how selling might impact your tax liability.

To decide whether to sell, conduct a thorough analysis of the advantages and disadvantages based on your situation.

Pros of Selling Now

High Market Demand: In a seller's market, you may receive multiple offers, potentially driving up the sale price.

Opportunity to Upgrade: Selling at a high price can give you more financial leverage for your next home.

Lifestyle Alignment: Moving to a home that better suits your needs can improve your quality of life.

Financial Flexibility: Cashing out equity can help pay down debt, invest, or fund other priorities.

Cons of Selling Now

High Replacement Costs: If the market is strong for sellers, it may also be competitive and expensive for buyers.

Emotional Stress: Packing up and relocating can be overwhelming.

Market Volatility: There's always a risk that market conditions could change, potentially affecting your plans.

Transaction Costs: Selling and buying come with significant expenses that can eat into profits.

KEY STEPS TO HELP YOU DECIDE

If you're still uncertain about selling, follow these steps to gain clarity:

Consult Professionals

Real Estate Agent: A knowledgeable agent, preferably a Realtor®, can guide you through market conditions, pricing strategies, and selling timelines.

Financial Advisor: If your decision to sell hinges on financial factors, an advisor can help you understand the long-term implications.

Tax Consultant: Ensure you're aware of potential tax liabilities.

Get a Comparative Market Analysis (CMA)

A real estate agent can provide a CMA, which compares your home to similar properties recently sold in your area. This report will give you a realistic estimate of your home's value and potential selling price.

Evaluate Your Timeline

Consider how quickly you need to sell. If timing is flexible, you can wait for favorable market conditions. If you're on a strict schedule, you may need to prioritize speed over maximizing profit.

Perform a Cost-Benefit Analysis

Use this exercise to weigh the financial and emotional benefits of selling against the costs. Include variables such as current market trends, selling expenses, and your future housing plans.

Test the Market

In some cases, you can list your home without a firm commitment to sell. If the response from buyers is strong, it may reaffirm your decision.

CONCLUSION

Selling your home is a significant personal decision shaped by numerous factors, including market dynamics and personal situations. While future outcomes are uncertain, assessing your motivations, financial status, and local trends will help you make a well-informed choice. Balancing profit, lifestyle aspirations, and emotional health is crucial.

Preparing Your Home for Sale: The Importance of First Impressions

Chapter Three

Selling a home is both an art and a science. At the heart of a successful home sale is the ability to price the property correctly—a balance that captures the home's value without overpricing it to the point of scaring off potential buyers. While market analysis and local trends play a significant role, the condition and presentation of your home are equally critical. Home staging, repairs, improvements, and overall aesthetics can transform your property, making it more appealing and, ultimately, more valuable.

Understanding the Role of Home Staging

Home staging is about creating a welcoming environment that allows potential buyers to visualize themselves living in your home. Staging doesn't necessarily require costly investments but focuses on enhancing the home's strengths and minimizing its flaws.

Why Staging Matters

Statistics consistently show that staged homes sell faster and at higher prices than their unstaged counterparts. Staging emphasizes the home's best features, making it stand out in listing photos and during showings. A well-staged home feels neutral yet inviting, enabling buyers to imagine their own furniture and lifestyle within its walls.

Practical Staging Tips

Depersonalize: Remove personal items such as family photos, unique collectibles, or bold artwork. Neutrality helps buyers focus on the home rather than your personality.

Maximize Space: Arrange furniture to make rooms appear larger and more functional. For example, use mirrors in smaller spaces to create an illusion of openness.

Add Warmth: Fresh flowers, cozy throws, or strategically placed rugs can make a home feel lived-in and welcoming.

Focus on Lighting: Ensure every room is well-lit with a mix of natural and artificial light. Replace dim bulbs and open curtains to let sunlight in.

REPAIRS AND IMPROVEMENTS THAT ADD VALUE

Buyers are typically more willing to pay a premium for a home that is move-in ready. Neglecting repairs or ignoring obvious flaws can lead to lower offers or longer time on the market.

Minor Repairs with Major Impact

Fix Leaky Faucets and Pipes: Plumbing issues can be a red flag for buyers, signaling potential larger problems.

Patch and Paint Walls: Cracks, stains, or outdated wall colors can make your home seem neglected. Opt for neutral colors that appeal to a broad audience.

Repair Flooring: Replace chipped tiles, refinish scratched hardwood floors, or replace worn-out carpets to create a polished look.

Strategic Home Improvements

While major renovations might not always yield a full return on investment, certain updates can significantly boost your home's appeal:

Kitchen Updates: A fresh coat of paint on cabinets, modern hardware, or new countertops can transform the heart of the home without requiring a full remodel.

Bathroom Refresh: Replace outdated fixtures, re-caulk bathtubs, and install new mirrors or lighting to create a spa-like feel.

Energy Efficiency Upgrades: Install energy-efficient windows, update insulation, or replace old appliances to attract eco-conscious buyers.

The exterior of your home is the first thing buyers see. A well-maintained, inviting curbside view sets the tone for the rest of the showing.

Key Elements of Curb Appeal

Landscaping: Trim overgrown bushes, mow the lawn, and plant seasonal flowers for a vibrant and cared-for look.

Front Door: Repaint or replace your front door with a color that complements your home's style. Add a stylish doormat or potted plants for extra charm.

Driveway and Walkways: Clean or reseal your driveway, and repair any cracks in walkways. Pressure washing can make a significant difference in appearance.

Exterior Lighting: Install or upgrade outdoor lights to highlight your home at night, ensuring it feels welcoming and secure.

Decluttering and Deep Cleaning

Clutter distracts buyers and makes spaces feel smaller, while cleanliness sends a signal of care and upkeep. Decluttering and deep cleaning are essential steps in preparing your home for sale.

Decluttering Basics

Organize Closets and Cabinets: Buyers often check storage spaces, so neat and organized closets make a good impression.

Remove Excess Furniture: Less is more when it comes to furniture. Remove bulky or unnecessary items to showcase space and flow.

Pack Personal Items: Consider packing away seasonal items, collections, and anything that doesn't contribute to a neutral aesthetic.

Deep Cleaning Essentials

Carpets and Floors: Hire professionals to clean carpets, and polish hardwood floors to remove years of wear and tear.

Kitchen and Bathrooms: Scrub every surface, including grout, behind appliances, and under sinks.

Windows and Mirrors: Clean windows and mirrors to let in more light and create a sparkling appearance.

Odor Removal: Neutralize odors from pets, cooking, or smoking to ensure your home smells fresh and inviting.

CONCLUSION

Pricing your home correctly involves much more than understanding the real estate market—it's about presenting a property that potential buyers will see as their future home. From staging and repairs to boosting curb appeal and embracing the power of deep cleaning, every effort contributes to maximizing your home's value. A well-prepared property not only attracts more buyers but also creates emotional connections, leading to competitive offers and faster sales. By investing time and effort into these strategies, you set the stage for success, ensuring that your home stands out in a crowded market and achieves the price it truly deserves.

"Making a first impression is a unique opportunity that does not come around again."
— Marcus E. Turner

Pricing Your Home Right: Strategy for Success

Chapter Four

Selling a home is one of the most significant financial transactions many individuals undertake, and the listing price plays a pivotal role in ensuring a successful and timely sale. Setting the right price is both an art and a science, requiring careful analysis of market conditions, comparable sales, and strategic planning. In this chapter, we'll explore how to set a competitive listing price, the importance of a Comparative Market Analysis (CMA), the influence of local market dynamics, and the potential risks of overpricing or underpricing a property.

THE IMPORTANCE OF PRICING YOUR HOME COMPETITIVELY

The listing price of your home determines its initial impression in the market. A well-priced home attracts potential buyers, generates interest, and may even spark a bidding war, maximizing your profit. Conversely, an improperly priced home can languish on the market, potentially leading to price reductions and diminished buyer interest.

A competitive price ensures:

Maximized exposure: More buyers are drawn to homes within their budget and perceived market value.

Quicker sales: Properties priced correctly tend to sell faster, reducing carrying costs like mortgage payments, property taxes, and maintenance.

Buyer confidence: A realistic price conveys trustworthiness and transparency, encouraging serious offers.

UNDERSTANDING COMPARATIVE MARKET ANALYSIS (CMA)

One of the most reliable tools for determining the right listing price is a

Comparative Market Analysis (CMA). A CMA evaluates the market value of a property by comparing it to similar homes recently sold in the same area. This analysis considers factors such as:

Size: Square footage, number of bedrooms, and bathrooms.

Condition: Renovations, upgrades, and overall property maintenance.

Location: Proximity to schools, amenities, transportation, and desirable neighborhoods.

Market trends: The average time homes stay on the market and whether prices are trending upward or downward.

Steps in Conducting a CMA

Identify comparable properties (comps): These should ideally be homes that are similar in size, age, and style, located within a close radius of the home being sold. Recent sales (within 3–6 months) provide the most accurate comparisons.

Adjust for differences: No two homes are identical. If a comparable property has a finished basement or additional square footage, adjustments are made to estimate the value difference.

Analyze current listings and expired listings: Active listings represent the competition, while expired listings often signal overpricing.

By leveraging a CMA, sellers can establish a fair market value for their home that aligns with buyer expectations and market realities.

THE ROLE OF LOCAL MARKET CONDITIONS

Local real estate market conditions have a significant impact on pricing strategy. Understanding whether the market favors buyers, sellers, or is balanced is critical to setting a competitive price.

Seller's Market

In a seller's market, demand exceeds supply. Homes tend to sell quickly, often above asking price. In this scenario:

Pricing slightly below market value can generate multiple offers, driving up the final sale price.

Aggressive pricing strategies may be more forgiving, but overpricing can still deter cautious buyers.

Buyer's Market

In a buyer's market, supply exceeds demand. Homes take longer to sell, and buyers have more negotiating power. Strategies include:

Pricing competitively or slightly below market value to stand out.

Highlighting the home's unique features and upgrades to justify the asking price.

Balanced Market

In a balanced market, supply and demand are relatively equal. Pricing accuracy is paramount because buyers and sellers have comparable leverage.

Monitoring local factors such as job growth, school ratings, new construction, and seasonal trends also informs pricing decisions. For example, homes typically sell faster in spring and summer due to increased buyer activity.

THE RISKS OF OVERPRICING A HOME

Overpricing a property is one of the most common mistakes sellers make, often due to emotional attachment or the desire to maximize profit. While it may seem like a safe strategy to leave room for negotiation, it can backfire significantly.

Negative Impacts of Overpricing

Reduced buyer interest: Buyers tend to skip overpriced homes, focusing instead on properties offering better perceived value.

Extended time on the market: Homes that sit on the market too long develop a stigma, leading buyers to assume something is wrong with the property.

Price reductions: Lowering the price after weeks or months of inactivity signals desperation, potentially leading to lowball offers.

Lost competitive edge: When similar homes in the area are priced lower, overpriced listings are overlooked, regardless of quality or features.

Example Scenario

A home worth $400,000 is listed at $450,000. After 60 days without offers, the seller reduces the price to $400,000. By this time, the property has been overlooked by many buyers who have moved on, and new offers may come in below $400,000 due to perceived seller desperation.

THE RISKS OF UNDERPRICING A HOME

While underpricing can generate a quick sale, it's essential to weigh the risks against the benefits.

Advantages of Underpricing

Attracting multiple buyers: A low price can create a sense of urgency, leading to competitive bidding and potentially driving up the final sale price.

Fast sale: In markets where time is critical, underpricing ensures the property doesn't linger on the market.

Potential Pitfalls

Leaving money on the table: If bidding wars fail to materialize, the seller may end up accepting a lower price than the home's actual value.

Buyer skepticism: A price significantly below market value can make buyers question the home's condition or hidden flaws.

Balanced Underpricing

Strategic underpricing works best in hot markets or when a property has unique features that appeal to a wide range of buyers.

STRATEGIES FOR SETTING THE RIGHT PRICE

Rely on data, not emotions: Focus on the home's market value rather than personal opinions or investment costs. Buyers base their decisions on facts, not sentimental attachments.

Work with a real estate professional: Experienced agents holding national credentials, including Pricing Strategy Advisor (PSA) and Seller Representative Specialist (SRS), have access to MLS data, market trends, and a broader understanding of buyer behavior. Their expertise is invaluable in pricing decisions.

Consider professional appraisals: If in doubt, a professional appraisal can provide an objective estimate of your home's value.

Price with room for negotiation: Setting a price slightly above market value allows for negotiation but should remain within a competitive range.

Monitor market feedback: If your home isn't receiving offers or showings within the first few weeks, it may be a sign that the price needs adjustment.

THE PSYCHOLOGY OF PRICING

Pricing is not just a numbers game; it's also about perception. Numbers ending in "9" (e.g., $399,000 instead of $400,000) often seem more attractive to buyers due to psychological pricing effects. Similarly, setting a price within a popular search range (e.g., $350,000 to $400,000) ensures your home appears in more buyer searches.

Setting the right price for your home is a critical step toward achieving a successful sale. By utilizing a Comparative Market Analysis, considering local market conditions, and understanding the risks of overpricing or underpricing, you can position your property to attract serious buyers and secure the best possible outcome.

Ultimately, the key to success lies in balancing data-driven decisions with a clear understanding of buyer psychology and market dynamics. Collaborating with a knowledgeable real estate professional ensures your pricing strategy aligns with your goals, helping you navigate the complexities of the real estate market with confidence.

WHY WORK WITH A REALTOR?

01

They negotiate on your behalf, ensuring you get the best deal.

02

They analyze market trends, providing you with valuable insights

03

They protect your interests in all legal and contractual aspects.

04

They save you time by streamlining your search.

05

They understand and help you navigate complex transactions.

06

They facilitate an overall straightforward, stress-free experience.

Figure 2

Marketing Your Home: Attracting the Right Buyers

Chapter Five

Selling a home is both an art and a science, requiring a well-thought-out marketing strategy to attract the right buyers. In a competitive real estate market, it is not enough to list a property and hope for the best. The right mix of traditional and contemporary marketing techniques can maximize your home's exposure, attract serious buyers, and achieve the best price. In this chapter, we'll explore effective strategies, emphasizing the importance of presenting your home in the best possible light.

START WITH PROFESSIONAL PHOTOGRAPHY

First impressions matter, and for many buyers, their first encounter with your property will be through photographs. Professional photography is an essential investment when marketing your home. High-quality images capture your property's best angles, highlight unique features, and make it stand out in a crowded marketplace.

Benefits: Professional photographers know how to use lighting, composition, and editing to make spaces appear larger, brighter, and more inviting.

Tips: Before the photoshoot, declutter and stage your home. Neutral decor, fresh flowers, and well-lit rooms enhance its appeal.

Buyers are increasingly drawn to virtual experiences, so consider adding virtual tours and 3D walkthroughs to your listing. These tools allow buyers to explore your home at their convenience, providing a realistic sense of the space without requiring an in-person visit.

CRAFT A COMPELLING ONLINE LISTING

Once you have stunning visuals, the next step is creating a compelling online listing. This is often the centerpiece of your marketing strategy.

Key Elements of an Effective Listing

- A catchy, descriptive headline (e.g., "Charming 3-Bedroom Cottage with Panoramic Views").
- A detailed yet concise property description, highlighting key features like remodeled kitchens, spacious gardens, or proximity to amenities.
- Clear, appealing images and videos.
- Accurate pricing to attract serious buyers and avoid discouraging offers.

Ensure your listing is available on popular platforms like Zillow, Realtor.com, and local Multiple Listing Services (MLS).

Effective SEO optimization is essential for crafting your description. Incorporating relevant keywords will enhance the visibility of your property in pertinent search results.

LEVERAGE SOCIAL MEDIA MARKETING

Social media has transformed the way homes are marketed. Platforms like Facebook, Instagram, YouTube, and TikTok allow you to target buyers in specific demographics and geographic areas.

Facebook: Create a dedicated post or ad featuring your home. Use Facebook Marketplace for additional visibility. You can target potential buyers based on their interests, behaviors, and location.

Instagram: Leverage Instagram Stories and Reels to showcase your home creatively. A quick, visually engaging video can capture attention and drive inquiries.

YouTube: Develop and distribute captivating and informative videos that creatively highlight your home. A brief, visually appealing video can attract interest and generate inquiries.

TikTok: Short, engaging videos highlighting unique features or offering "home tours" can attract a younger demographic.

Consistency is key. Posting regularly and engaging with comments can boost the visibility of your home, ensuring it reaches the right buyers.

UTILIZE TRADITIONAL MARKETING METHODS

While digital strategies dominate, traditional methods remain highly effective, particularly for reaching buyers who value personal connections.

Open Houses: Open houses provide buyers with a chance to experience your home firsthand. A well-staged, inviting atmosphere encourages buyers to imagine themselves living in the space.

Mailers and Flyers: Direct mail campaigns target potential buyers in your area or specific demographics. Use eye-catching designs and concise messaging to pique interest. Highlight any recent renovations or unique features.

For Sale Signs: A classic, yet effective strategy. Ensure the sign is professionally designed, includes a phone number or QR code, and is placed in a visible location.

EMAIL AND TEXT MARKETING

Direct communication through email and text campaigns is another powerful tool.

Email Campaigns: It is essential to work with a Realtor® who possesses email lists of prospective buyers, real estate agents, and investors. They should recognize the significance of dispatching targeted emails that feature compelling subject lines, high-quality visuals, links to virtual tours, and information about open house events.

Text Messaging: Make sure your Realtor® utilizes SMS to provide prompt and direct notifications regarding price reductions, open houses, or new listings, including a clear call-to-action.

PARTNER WITH A SKILLED REAL ESTATE AGENT

A knowledgeable and experienced real estate agent is an invaluable partner in marketing your home. They can:

- Provide insights into market trends to position your home competitively.
- Tap into their professional network of potential buyers and agents.
- Negotiate offers to ensure you get the best value.

Agents often have access to exclusive marketing tools, such as private MLS databases and industry events, that can amplify your home's visibility.

FOCUS ON HOME STAGING

Staging your home goes beyond cleaning and decluttering; it involves arranging furniture, decor, and lighting to appeal to buyers' emotions. Staged homes sell faster and often for higher prices than unstaged ones.

DIY Staging Tips

- Neutralize the space by removing personal items like family photos.
- Highlight focal points in rooms, such as fireplaces or large windows.
- Use mirrors to create the illusion of space and light.

For a professional touch, consider hiring a staging company that specializes in creating magazine-worthy interiors.

ENGAGE WITH NICHE MARKETS

If your home has unique features, target niche buyers who would value them. For instance:

Eco-Friendly Buyers: Highlight energy-efficient appliances, solar panels, or sustainable materials used in construction.

Luxury Buyers: Emphasize upscale amenities like smart home technology, gourmet kitchens, or spa-like bathrooms.

Families: Showcase proximity to schools, playgrounds, and community centers.

Tailor your marketing message to resonate with these specific audiences.

Utilize Video and Drone Marketing

Incorporating video marketing into your strategy can significantly enhance buyer engagement. Drone footage, in particular, provides stunning aerial views of your property and its surroundings, making it especially appealing for homes with large lots or scenic locations.

Content Ideas

- A narrated walkthrough, guiding viewers through the home and highlighting its best features.
- Drone shots of the neighborhood, showcasing parks, schools, or nearby attractions.

Upload these videos to YouTube, social media, and your online listing for maximum exposure.

Offer Incentives to Buyers and Agents

Sometimes, offering incentives can set your home apart and attract serious buyers.

For Buyers: Consider covering part of the closing costs or offering a home warranty.

For Agents: Offering a competitive commission can encourage other realtors to prioritize your property with their clients.

Once your home is on the market, regularly review your marketing performance. If interest seems low, consider adjusting your pricing, updating your listing photos, or exploring additional platforms. Work closely with your agent to stay informed about buyer feedback and adapt as needed.

CONCLUSION

Marketing your home effectively is about showcasing its best qualities and reaching the right audience. By combining traditional and contemporary strategies—professional photography, online listings, social media, open houses, and direct mail—you can create a comprehensive approach that attracts serious buyers.

Remember, the goal isn't just to sell quickly but to achieve the best price for your property. With the right strategy and professional support, your home will capture the attention it deserves, making the selling process a rewarding experience.

Know your audience and
tailor your messaging

Offer a unique
value proposition

Focus on building
customer loyalty

6 TIPS
For Marketing
Success

Use social media
to engage with your
audience

Create visually
appealing content that
grabs attention

Use storytelling to
create an emotional
connection

Figure 3

Negotiating Offers: Getting the Best Deal

Chapter Six

Negotiating offers in the real estate market is both an art and a science. For sellers, the process of evaluating and responding to offers can significantly impact the final outcome of a sale. Whether navigating a buyer's, seller's, or balanced market, understanding how to review, counter, and negotiate offers is crucial. This chapter provides practical advice to help sellers secure the best possible deal while maintaining a professional and effective negotiation process.

UNDERSTANDING THE MARKET CONTEXT

Before diving into negotiations, it's essential to understand the market conditions. The dynamics of a buyer's, seller's, or balanced market influence the strategies you should employ:

Seller's Market: In this environment, demand exceeds supply. Homes sell quickly, often with multiple offers, and sellers have the advantage. Negotiation strategies should leverage this position to secure favorable terms.

Buyer's Market: With more homes available than buyers, the power shifts to buyers. Sellers may need to be more flexible and creative to make their property stand out.

Balanced Market: Supply and demand are relatively equal, leading to more neutral negotiations. Both parties must focus on fair terms and value.

Understanding the market type helps you set realistic expectations and tailor your negotiation approach.

When an offer arrives, the first step is careful evaluation. Beyond the purchase price, consider other components that can impact the deal:

Price: The headline figure is critical, but it's not the only factor to consider. Look for offers that align with your asking price and market value.

Financing Terms: Determine if the buyer is pre-approved for a mortgage or offering cash. Cash offers often close faster and have fewer contingencies, making them highly desirable.

Contingencies: These include inspections, appraisals, and financing clauses. Contingencies protect the buyer but can introduce uncertainty for the seller. Fewer contingencies generally mean a smoother transaction.

Concessions: These include buyer-broker commission, closing cost assistance, repairs, home warranties, or price reductions to enhance affordability and ease the purchasing process.

Closing Timeline: Ensure the proposed timeline aligns with your needs. Some buyers may offer flexibility, which can be advantageous if you need time to relocate.

Earnest Money Deposit: A higher earnest money deposit signals serious intent from the buyer. It also provides security if the buyer backs out without a valid reason.

Additional Requests: Buyers may include requests for specific inclusions (e.g., appliances or furniture). These requests can affect the overall value of the offer.

Once all aspects are reviewed, categorize offers into strong, moderate, and weak to prioritize your response strategy.

Counteroffers allow you to refine an offer to better meet your expectations. This process involves careful balancing to retain the buyer's interest while improving terms for the seller.

Identify Priorities

Decide what matters most—price, timeline, or reduced contingencies. Communicate these priorities clearly to your agent, who will draft the counteroffer.

Set a Firm Yet Reasonable Tone

Avoid overly aggressive counters that could alienate the buyer. Instead, aim for a tone that reflects collaboration and mutual benefit.

Tweak Specific Terms

- Increase the price if the initial offer is below your expectations.
- Adjust the closing timeline if it doesn't suit your needs.
- Reduce contingencies or request a higher earnest money deposit to minimize risks.

Time Sensitivity

Include an expiration date in your counteroffer. This creates urgency and prevents buyers from delaying decisions while exploring other options. Remember, counteroffers are not just about rejecting terms but finding common ground that satisfies both parties.

NEGOTIATING THE BEST TERMS

Negotiating offers is a dynamic process that requires preparation, adaptability, and effective communication. Here are strategies to help sellers secure the best terms:

Leverage the Market Conditions

In a Seller's Market: Highlight the property's competitive position. If multiple offers are on the table, let buyers know they are competing. This often encourages better terms or escalation clauses.

In a Buyer's Market: Offer incentives to stand out. For instance, consider paying for a home warranty or including appliances to sweeten the deal.

In a Balanced Market: Focus on fair value. Emphasize the home's unique features and the fairness of your counteroffer.

Stay Flexible but Firm

Flexibility can foster goodwill, but know your non-negotiables. For instance:

- Be willing to adjust the closing date if the buyer requests it.
- Stand firm on the price or contingencies that protect your interests.

Communicate Clearly

Use your Realtor® as a mediator to convey responses profession-ally and unemotionally. Agents can frame counteroffers in ways that highlight their value without alienating the buyer.

Avoid Common Pitfalls

Overpricing: Overestimating your property's worth can drive buyers away.

Neglecting Small Wins: Focusing solely on the price may cause you to overlook valuable concessions, such as a faster closing or fewer contingencies.

Dragging the Process: Prolonged negotiations can frustrate buyers, increasing the risk they'll walk away.

STRATEGIES FOR NAVIGATING MULTIPLE OFFERS

Receiving multiple offers is a favorable position for sellers but requires careful management to maximize outcomes. Consider these tactics:

Request Best and Final Offers: Inform buyers to submit their highest and best offers by a specific deadline. This creates urgency and encourages competitive bids.

Weigh Financial Strength: Beyond the price, evaluate the buyer's financial capability. A slightly lower cash offer might be more reliable than a higher financed offer.

Use an Escalation Clause: Encourage buyers to include escalation clauses, which automatically increase their offer up to a specified limit if competing bids exceed theirs.

Communicate Transparently: Be honest with buyers about the competition, but avoid disclosing exact terms of other offers to maintain ethical practices.

Key Considerations in Buyer's Markets

Negotiations in buyer's markets require sellers to be more accommodating to close deals. Strategies include:

Highlight Unique Features: Emphasize aspects of your home that differentiate it from others, such as renovations, energy-efficient appliances, or location perks.

Offer Concessions: Consider covering some closing costs or offering credits for repairs to attract buyers.

Be Open to Contingencies: While fewer contingencies are ideal, accepting reasonable ones may make your offer more appealing to buyers.

Maintaining Professionalism

Negotiations can become emotional, especially when sellers have a personal attachment to the property. To maintain professionalism:

Separate Emotions from Business: Focus on the transaction's financial and practical aspects rather than emotional ties.

Rely on Your Agent: Let your agent handle communications and provide objective advice throughout the process.

Stay Patient: Good deals often take time. Avoid rushing decisions out of frustration or anxiety.

Closing the Deal

Once both parties agree on terms, the process moves to the contract stage. At this point:

Review the Agreement Thoroughly: Ensure all negotiated terms are accurately reflected in the contract.

Fulfill Obligations Promptly: Complete any agreed-upon repairs or disclosures to avoid delays.

Stay Prepared for Last-Minute Negotiations: Buyers may request concessions during inspections or before closing. Assess these requests carefully and respond strategically.

Conclusion

Negotiating real estate offers is a skillful balancing act requiring preparation, market knowledge, and effective communication. Sellers who understand the nuances of reviewing offers, crafting counteroffers, and adapting to market conditions can maximize their outcomes. Whether in a buyer's, seller's, or balanced market, the key is to remain flexible, professional, and focused on achieving a deal that aligns with your goals. With the right approach, negotiation becomes a pathway to securing the best possible deal.

Understanding the Closing Process: From Offer to Sold

Chapter Seven

The journey from an accepted offer to the official transfer of property ownership is one of the most critical stages in a real estate transaction. This process, commonly referred to as "closing," ensures all legal, financial, and logistical requirements are met to finalize the sale. Whether you're a first-time seller or an experienced one, understanding the closing process can alleviate stress and help you stay prepared for each step. In this chapter, we will outline the key components of the closing process, including inspections, appraisals, title checks, and the seller's responsibilities.

OFFER ACCEPTANCE

Once a buyer makes an offer and the seller accepts it, a legally binding purchase agreement is signed by both parties. This contract sets the terms of the sale, including the agreed-upon price, contingencies, timelines, and closing date. For the closing process to proceed smoothly, the seller must carefully review and adhere to the terms outlined in the agreement.

EARNEST MONEY DEPOSIT

Buyers typically submit an earnest money deposit shortly after the offer is accepted. This deposit demonstrates the buyer's serious intent to purchase the property. The funds are held in an escrow account and applied toward the buyer's down payment or closing costs unless the transaction falls through due to unmet contingencies.

HOME INSPECTION

One of the most significant contingencies in most real estate transactions is the home inspection. This involves a professional inspector evaluating the property for structural integrity, safety hazards, and necessary repairs.

For sellers, this is a critical moment to ensure the property is in satisfactory condition. If issues arise, buyers may request repairs or negotiate for credits. To minimize surprises, some sellers choose to conduct a pre-inspection before listing the home. This proactive step can identify and address potential concerns ahead of time, reducing delays in the closing process.

APPRAISAL

If the buyer is financing the purchase with a mortgage, the lender will order an appraisal to determine the property's fair market value. The appraisal protects the lender by ensuring the property is worth the loan amount.

For sellers, the appraisal can either affirm the agreed price or introduce complications. If the appraisal comes in lower than the purchase price, the buyer may renegotiate or back out, depending on the contract's contingencies. Preparing the property to look its best—cleaning, staging, and addressing visible maintenance issues—can positively influence the appraisal outcome.

TITLE SEARCH AND INSURANCE

A clean title is essential for a smooth closing. The title search confirms that the seller has legal ownership of the property and uncovers any liens, disputes, or encumbrances that could hinder the transfer.

The title company or attorney conducting the search will issue a preliminary title report for review. If any issues are found, such as unpaid property taxes or conflicting ownership claims, the seller must resolve them before closing. Additionally, buyers typically purchase title insurance to protect against future claims, while sellers may provide a warranty deed guaranteeing clear ownership transfer.

Securing Financing

While securing financing is primarily the buyer's responsibility, sellers should be aware of this step's significance. Lenders require buyers to submit financial documents, verify creditworthiness, and meet loan conditions before issuing final approval. Delays in this stage can impact the closing timeline, so sellers should remain flexible while ensuring all seller-related requirements are promptly met.

Final Walkthrough

Typically conducted 24 to 48 hours before closing, the final walkthrough allows buyers to ensure the property's condition matches the agreement's terms. Buyers check that agreed-upon repairs are completed, fixtures included in the sale remain in place, and no new damage has occurred since the initial inspection.

Sellers should prepare for the walkthrough by addressing repair requests, removing personal belongings, and leaving the property clean and ready for move-in. A seamless walkthrough minimizes the chances of last-minute disputes or delays.

Closing Disclosure and Documentation

Buyers receive a Closing Disclosure at least three days before the closing date, outlining final loan terms, closing costs, and other financial details. While this document is primarily for the buyer's review, sellers should also confirm they understand their net proceeds, which are detailed in the seller's statement.

Sellers must also provide necessary documents, including a valid government-issued ID, the original property deed, and any warranties or manuals for appliances included in the sale. Timely preparation of these documents ensures a smooth closing process.

Closing day marks the culmination of the entire process. Both parties meet to sign final documents, which may include the deed, settlement statement, and loan agreements. The buyer pays closing costs, and the seller receives the net proceeds from the sale.

In some cases, sellers may not need to attend the closing in person, especially if they've granted power of attorney to their agent or attorney. Regardless, sellers should confirm that all documentation is accurate and complete to avoid complications.

Handover of Keys and Possession

Once the sale is officially closed and the funds are transferred, the seller hands over the keys, garage door openers, and any other access devices to the buyer. Sellers should ensure the property is vacated by the agreed possession date, leaving behind only items specified in the contract.

Tips for Sellers to Ensure a Smooth Closing

Stay Organized: Keep all documents, such as inspection reports, repair receipts, and title documents, readily accessible.

Communicate Openly: Maintain clear communication with your Realtor®, attorney, and buyer to address questions or concerns promptly.

Fulfill Contingencies: Ensure all contingencies, such as repairs or removal of liens, are completed within the agreed timeline.

Prepare the Property: Leave the home clean and free of personal items to create a positive impression during the final walkthrough.

Be Flexible with Timelines: While frustrating, delays in financing or other stages are common. Patience and flexibility can help navigate these challenges without jeopardizing the sale.

The closing process involves multiple steps, each requiring attention to detail and proactive communication. From inspections and appraisals to title searches and final walkthroughs, every element is designed to ensure a fair and seamless transaction for both parties. Sellers who understand these steps and take the necessary actions to prepare can facilitate a smooth closing experience, ultimately achieving their goal of transferring ownership successfully.

By staying informed, organized, and cooperative, sellers can navigate the closing process with confidence and peace of mind, turning the stress of selling into the satisfaction of a completed transaction.

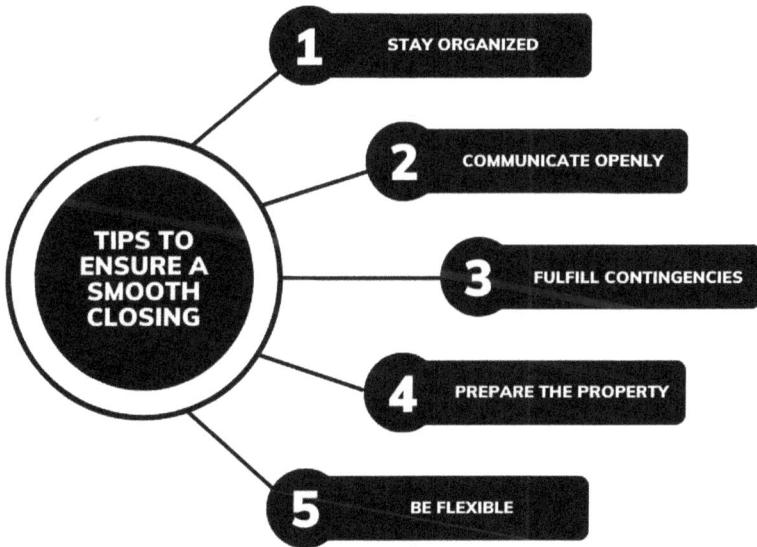

TIPS TO ENSURE A SMOOTH CLOSING

1 STAY ORGANIZED

2 COMMUNICATE OPENLY

3 FULFILL CONTINGENCIES

4 PREPARE THE PROPERTY

5 BE FLEXIBLE

Figure 4

Avoiding Common Pitfalls: Mistakes to Watch Out For

Chapter Eight

Selling a home can be one of the most significant financial and emotional transactions of your life. While it can be an exciting chapter, the process can also feel overwhelming, especially if you're not prepared. There are numerous common mistakes sellers make, and these pitfalls can lead to stress, delayed sales, or even financial losses. The good news is that with a little planning and awareness, you can sidestep these errors and ensure a smoother, more profitable sale. Let's explore some of the most common pitfalls and provide actionable tips to avoid them.

OVERPRICING THE HOME

One of the most common mistakes sellers make is overpricing their property. While it's natural to want the best possible price for your home, setting the price too high can deter potential buyers and prolong your time on the market.

How to Avoid It

Work with a knowledgeable real estate agent to conduct a comprehensive market analysis. This will help you understand what similar homes in your area have sold for and set a competitive, realistic price. Remember, an overpriced home can become "stale" in the market, forcing you to make price reductions later.

NEGLECTING NECESSARY REPAIRS AND UPDATES

Many sellers underestimate the importance of addressing repairs or making cosmetic updates before listing. Buyers often interpret visible issues, like peeling paint or leaky faucets, as signs of neglect, which can decrease your home's perceived value.

How to Avoid It

Before listing, conduct a thorough walk-through or hire a home inspector to identify potential issues. Fix minor repairs and consider low-cost improvements, like repainting walls or updating light fixtures, to enhance your home's appeal.

Ignoring Curb Appeal

First impressions matter. A neglected exterior—overgrown landscaping, faded paint, or a cracked driveway—can turn off buyers before they even step inside.

How to Avoid It

Invest time and resources in boosting curb appeal. Trim bushes, plant flowers, clean the driveway, and repaint the front door. These small investments can make a big difference in attracting buyers.

Skimping on Staging

Empty or cluttered homes can make it hard for buyers to visualize themselves living in the space. Similarly, overly personalized decor can distract from the home's features.

How to Avoid It

Consider professional staging or virtual staging services to make your home feel welcoming and spacious. If hiring a stager isn't in the budget, declutter and depersonalize by removing family photos, excessive furniture, and bold decor.

Not Marketing the Home Effectively

Even the most beautiful home won't sell if potential buyers don't know it's available. Poor-quality photos, limited online exposure, or lack of marketing strategy can hurt your chances.

How to Avoid It

Partner with a real estate agent who uses professional photography, detailed listings, and a strong online marketing strategy. Your home should be listed on major real estate platforms, shared on social media, and even featured in virtual tours to attract the widest audience possible.

BEING INFLEXIBLE WITH SHOWINGS

Selling a home requires accommodating potential buyers, and being too rigid with showing schedules can discourage interested parties.

How to Avoid It

Keep your home show-ready and be as flexible as possible with viewing times. This might mean leaving the house at short notice or accommodating evening and weekend showings, but the effort can pay off in securing a sale.

OVERLOOKING CLOSING COSTS

Sellers often focus on their potential profit and forget about the costs associated with closing a sale. These can include agent commissions, transfer taxes, and potential concessions for the buyer.

How to Avoid It

Before listing your home, have a clear understanding of all potential costs involved in the sale. Work with your agent to calculate net proceeds so you can avoid surprises at the closing table.

LETTING EMOTIONS TAKE OVER

Your home likely holds sentimental value, but letting emotions influence your decisions can lead to unrealistic pricing or difficulty negotiating.

How to Avoid It

Treat the sale as a business transaction. Rely on your agent's expertise and focus on market data rather than personal feelings. Remember, your goal is to sell the house for a fair price and move forward.

SELLING AT THE WRONG TIME

The timing of your sale can have a significant impact on the outcome. Listing during a slow market or poor economic conditions can result in a lower sale price.

How to Avoid It

Research the local real estate market and consider seasonal trends. In many areas, spring and early summer are peak times for selling homes, but a knowledgeable agent can help you determine the best time based on your specific market conditions.

NOT VETTING BUYERS PROPERLY

Accepting an offer without confirming the buyer's financial qualifications can lead to deals falling through, wasting valuable time.

How to Avoid It

Only entertain offers from pre-approved buyers. Your agent can help verify proof of funds or mortgage pre-approval letters to ensure the buyer is serious and capable of completing the purchase.

FAILING TO DISCLOSE ISSUES

Sellers sometimes think that withholding information about the property's problems will make the sale smoother, but undisclosed issues can lead to legal troubles later.

How to Avoid It

Be transparent about your home's condition and disclose any known issues upfront. Buyers will likely conduct their own inspection, and honesty builds trust. In some cases, addressing these issues proactively can even strengthen your negotiating position.

MISJUDGING THE MARKET

Assuming that your home will sell quickly because of general trends or anecdotal experiences can backfire. Each market and property is unique.

How to Avoid It

Research market conditions thoroughly or rely on your agent's expertise. Understand whether it's a buyer's or seller's market and adjust your pricing and expectations accordingly.

GOING FSBO WITHOUT RESEARCH

Some sellers attempt to sell their home without a real estate agent to save on commission costs, but this can lead to undervaluing the home, marketing missteps, or legal errors.

How to Avoid It

If you choose to go the For Sale By Owner (FSBO) route, educate yourself on local real estate laws, pricing strategies, and marketing techniques. Alternatively, consider working with an agent who can maximize your profits and minimize stress.

NEGLECTING TO PREPARE FINANCIALLY FOR THE NEXT STEP

Selling your home is just one part of the process. Many sellers don't plan for the financial aspects of buying their next home or relocating.

How to Avoid It

Have a clear plan for where you'll live after the sale. Consult with a mortgage broker or financial advisor to understand your purchasing power for a new home and create a transition budget.

RUSHING THE PROCESS

Sometimes, sellers rush to list their home without taking the time to properly prepare. This can lead to lower offers or unnecessary stress during negotiations.

How to Avoid It

Take the time to prepare your home, research the market, and create a thoughtful selling strategy. A well-planned sale is more likely to result in a favorable outcome.

CONCLUSION

Selling a home is a complex process, but avoiding these common pitfalls can make it far more manageable and rewarding. By pricing your home correctly, preparing it for showings, and working with experienced professionals, you can minimize stress and maximize your profit. Whether it's your first time selling or you're a seasoned homeowner, staying informed and proactive will help you achieve your goals and move on to the next chapter with confidence.

Don't Get Caught in a Web When You Sell

Avoid the Common Pitfalls of Selling

Tax Implications of Selling Your Home

Chapter Nine

Selling a home is a significant financial decision that carries potential tax implications. While the prospect of a profit from selling your home is exciting, it's essential to understand the tax consequences that may come with it. Homeowners must evaluate both the benefits, such as capital gains exclusions, and the costs, including closing fees and agent commissions. A well-informed approach ensures you can maximize your net proceeds and avoid unpleasant surprises when tax season rolls around.

CAPITAL GAINS TAX ON HOME SALES

One of the most critical tax considerations when selling a home is the capital gains tax. This tax applies to the profit—or gain—you make from selling your property. The formula for calculating this gain is:

Capital Gain = Selling Price − (Purchase Price + Cost of Improvements + Selling Expenses)

The good news is that many homeowners qualify for a capital gains tax exclusion under the Internal Revenue Code Section 121. This exclusion can significantly reduce or even eliminate your taxable gain.

Eligibility for Capital Gains Tax Exclusion

To qualify for the capital gains tax exclusion, you must meet the following conditions:

Ownership and Use Test: You must have owned and lived in the home as your primary residence for at least two of the five years preceding the sale.

Exclusion Amount: If you meet the criteria, you can exclude up to $250,000 of capital gains if you're single or $500,000 if you're married and filing jointly.

Examples of Tax Savings

Imagine you purchased a home 10 years ago for $300,000 and spent $50,000 on major improvements. You sell it for $600,000 today. Your capital gain is calculated as:

Capital Gain=$600,000−($300,000+$50,000)=$250,000

If you're single, this entire gain could be excluded from taxation under the $250,000 limit. For a married couple, any gain up to $500,000 would be tax-free.

Exceptions to the Exclusion

Certain situations might still allow partial exclusion of capital gains, such as selling your home due to a change in employment, health reasons, or unforeseen circumstances. The IRS provides guidelines to determine the exclusion amount in these cases.

COSTS ASSOCIATED WITH SELLING YOUR HOME

While capital gains exclusions can alleviate tax burdens, homeowners should also account for the numerous costs associated with selling a home. These expenses reduce the amount of profit you ultimately keep.

Closing Costs

Closing costs are expenses incurred to finalize the sale of your home. Common closing costs include:

Title Insurance: Protects against legal disputes over property ownership.

Escrow Fees: Charges for managing the transfer of funds between buyer and seller.

Transfer Taxes: Fees imposed by state or local governments on the sale of real estate.

Closing costs can range from 1% to 3% of the home's sale price. For a $500,000 home, this could amount to $5,000 to $15,000, which directly reduces your net proceeds.

Real Estate Agent Commissions
If you work with a real estate agent to list your home, you'll typically pay a commission based on the sale price of your home. The commission rate is consistently open to negotiation. Typically, a real estate agent will present a selection of services for clients to select from.

Seller Concessions
Seller concessions can play a significant role in real estate transactions. They refer to the financial incentives offered by sellers to attract buyers, such as covering buyer-broker commissions, closing costs or providing credits for repairs. These concessions can make properties more appealing, facilitate negotiations, and ultimately help close deals in competitive markets.

Repairs and Staging Costs
Preparing your home for sale often requires investments in repairs, renovations, and staging. Common expenses include:

* Fixing structural or cosmetic issues.
* Painting, landscaping, and deep cleaning.
* Renting furniture or decor to make your home more appealing to buyers.

These costs can vary widely but may add up to several thousand dollars, depending on the condition of your home and market expectations.

Mortgage Payoff and Prepayment Penalties
If you still owe money on your mortgage, the outstanding balance will be deducted from the proceeds at closing. Additionally, some loans include prepayment penalties for paying off the mortgage early, which could further reduce your profit.

Although selling your home generates costs, some of these expenses may be deductible, which can help lower your overall tax liability.

Selling Expenses

Selling expenses, such as advertising, legal fees, and real estate commissions, are generally deductible from your capital gain when calculating taxable profit. This deduction can substantially reduce your tax burden.

Home Improvements

Certain home improvement costs can be added to your property's basis, thereby reducing your capital gain. To qualify, the improvements must be significant, such as adding a new roof, remodeling a kitchen, or building a deck. Routine maintenance and repairs, like fixing a leaky faucet, don't count.

Moving Expenses

If you're selling your home because of a job relocation, you may qualify to deduct moving expenses, provided the move meets the IRS's distance and time tests. These deductions can cover the cost of transporting belongings and traveling to the new location.

Tax Implications for Second Homes and Investment Properties

The tax rules differ significantly for second homes and investment properties. These properties do not qualify for the capital gains tax exclusion available for primary residences.

Second Homes

If you sell a second home, such as a vacation property, the profit is subject to capital gains tax without the benefit of exclusions. However, if you've converted a second home into your primary residence for at least two of the past five years, you might be eligible for the exclusion.

Investment Properties

For rental or investment properties, the capital gains tax applies to any profit from the sale. Additionally, you must consider depreciation recapture, which taxes the depreciation you claimed while renting out the property. This can significantly impact your tax liability.

One strategy to defer taxes on investment property sales is a 1031 exchange, which allows you to reinvest the proceeds into a similar property without recognizing immediate gains. While this approach requires careful planning and adherence to strict timelines, it can be a valuable tool for real estate investors.

TAX IMPLICATIONS OF LOSSES ON HOME SALES

While capital gains are taxable, losses on the sale of your primary residence are not deductible. However, losses on investment properties or second homes may be deductible under certain circumstances. It's essential to consult a tax professional to explore potential deductions and ensure compliance with IRS rules.

RECORD-KEEPING FOR TAX PURPOSES

To accurately calculate your gain or loss and take advantage of available deductions, it's crucial to maintain thorough records related to your home. Important documents include:

- The original purchase agreement.
- Receipts for home improvements.
- Records of closing costs from both the purchase and sale of the property.

These records will help substantiate your claims if the IRS audits your tax return.

STATE AND LOCAL TAXES

In addition to federal taxes, some states impose taxes on home sales, such as:

- Transfer Taxes: Levied on the transfer of property ownership.
- State Capital Gains Taxes: Some states tax capital gains in addition to federal rates.

Understanding your state's tax laws is vital to accurately estimating your total tax liability.

CONCLUSION

Selling your home has far-reaching financial and tax implications. While the capital gains tax exclusion offers substantial benefits for many home-owners, various costs and conditions must also be considered. By under-standing the tax rules, accounting for selling expenses, and keeping detailed records, you can navigate the process more confidently and maximize your net proceeds.

For complex situations, such as selling investment properties or dealing with unique tax scenarios, consulting with a tax advisor or real estate professional is highly recommended. A proactive approach ensures that you're prepared for the tax implications and can make the most of your home sale.

"Taking a proactive stance not only prepares you for potential tax implications but also empowers you to maximize the benefits of your home sale."

— Marcus E. Turner

Working with a Realtor®: How to Choose the Right Professional

Chapter Ten

Buying or selling a home is one of the most significant financial decisions many people make in their lifetime. The process can be complex, emotional, and time-consuming. That's where a Realtor® comes in. A qualified Realtor® serves as your advocate, guide, and negotiator throughout the real estate process, ensuring that your interests are protected and your goals are met. However, selecting the right professional is critical to your success. This article explores the benefits of hiring a Realtor®, provides tips on how to choose one who aligns with your needs, and explains what to expect from their services.

THE BENEFITS OF HIRING A REALTOR®

Expertise and Market Knowledge

Realtors® are licensed professionals trained in the intricacies of real estate transactions. They bring a wealth of knowledge about market trends, neighborhood values, and local regulations. Whether you're buying or selling, a Realtor® can offer invaluable insights to help you make informed decisions.

For Sellers: Realtors® provide data-driven pricing strategies, ensuring you set a competitive price. They also advise on how to prepare your home to attract buyers and maximize your return.

For Buyers: Realtors® can identify properties that meet your criteria, often before they hit the market. They can guide you through financing options and help you understand the true value of a home.

Access to Resources

Realtors® have access to the Multiple Listing Service (MLS), a comprehensive database of homes for sale. This allows them to provide up-to-date and accurate information. They also have established networks with other professionals, such as inspectors, appraisers, and contractors, which can streamline the buying or selling process.

Negotiation Skills

A skilled Realtor® acts as your negotiator, advocating for your best interests. Whether it's negotiating the purchase price, contingencies, or repairs, their experience can save you money and stress.

Legal and Transactional Guidance

Real estate transactions involve extensive paperwork and legal obligations. A Realtor® ensures all documents are completed accurately and on time, reducing the risk of costly mistakes or legal issues.

Emotional Support

Buying or selling a home can be emotional, especially when dealing with financial pressures or family dynamics. A Realtor® provides a steady hand and objective perspective, helping you stay focused on your goals.

HOW TO CHOOSE THE RIGHT REALTOR®

Selecting the right Realtor® is a personal decision that can significantly impact your experience. Here's how to find one who aligns with your goals:

Start with Referrals and Research

Ask for Recommendations: Friends, family, and colleagues who've had positive experiences with a Realtor® are excellent resources. They can provide insight into the professional's work ethic, communication style, and effectiveness.

Online Reviews and Ratings: Websites like Zillow, Realtor.com, and Google often feature client reviews. Look for consistent patterns of satisfied customers and positive outcomes.

Verify Credentials and Experience

Licensing and Membership: Ensure the professional is a licensed Realtor® (not all real estate agents are Realtors®) and a member of the

National Association of Realtors® (NAR). Membership indicates adherence to a strict code of ethics.

Specializations: Some Realtors® specialize in certain types of properties, such as luxury homes, first-time buyers, or investment properties. Choose one whose expertise matches your needs.

Track Record: Ask about their recent sales history and experience in your target area. A seasoned Realtor® often has deeper market insights and a stronger network.

Interview Potential Candidates

Ask questions like:

- How long have you been in real estate?
- What areas do you specialize in?
- How will you market my home (for sellers)?
- How will you help me find the right property (for buyers)?
- What is your availability for showings or consultations?

Assess Compatibility

A Realtor®-client relationship requires trust and communication. Look for someone whose personality and communication style align with yours. Do they listen to your needs and concerns? Are they responsive and proactive?

Understand Their Commission and Fees

Realtors® generally receive a commission based on a percentage of the sale price of a home. For sellers, engaging a real estate agent to list your property allows for negotiation of the commission rate. Usually, agents provide a range of services for clients to choose from. It is important to discuss the commission structure at the outset and clarify which services are included.

Once you've chosen a Realtor®, it's essential to understand their responsibilities and how they'll support you. Here's an overview of what to expect:

Comprehensive Services

For Sellers: Your Realtor® will conduct a market analysis, help stage your home, list it on the MLS, and create a marketing strategy. They'll coordinate showings, negotiate offers, and manage closing details.

For Buyers: They'll help you define your needs and budget, identify suitable properties, schedule viewings, and guide you through offers, inspections, and closing.

Clear Communication

A good Realtor® keeps you informed at every stage. They should provide regular updates, explain processes clearly, and answer your questions promptly. Open communication builds trust and ensures a smoother experience.

Professionalism and Ethical Standards

As members of the NAR, Realtors® must adhere to a code of ethics. This includes prioritizing your interests, maintaining confidentiality, and avoiding conflicts of interest.

Problem-Solving Skills

Real estate transactions often encounter challenges, such as appraisal discrepancies or inspection issues. A skilled Realtor® proactively addresses these problems and seeks solutions that align with your goals.

MAXIMIZING VALUE FROM YOUR REALTOR®

To ensure you get the most from your Realtor®, take an active role in the process. Here are some tips:

Clearly Define Your Goals

Be upfront about your priorities, whether it's a quick sale, finding a fixer-upper, or relocating to a specific neighborhood. The more your Realtor® understands your objectives, the better they can serve you.

Be Open to Their Expertise

While you may have ideas about pricing or marketing, trust your Realtor's® recommendations. Their advice is based on market data and experience.

Provide Honest Feedback

During consultations or showings, share your likes and dislikes openly. This helps your Realtor® refine their approach and tailor their services to your needs.

Stay Engaged

While your Realtor® handles many tasks, your involvement is still crucial. Review documents thoroughly, attend inspections, and stay responsive to their communications.

Evaluate Their Performance

Throughout the process, assess whether your Realtor® is meeting your expectations. If issues arise, address them promptly. Most Realtors® are committed to delivering excellent service and will appreciate constructive feedback.

CONCLUSION

Hiring the right Realtor® is a game-changer when navigating the real estate market. Their expertise, resources, and dedication can save you time, money, and stress while ensuring a successful transaction. By researching candidates, assessing their compatibility, and understanding what to expect, you can find a professional who aligns with your goals and delivers exceptional value.

Remember, a great Realtor® is more than just a facilitator—they're a partner in one of life's most significant endeavors. Choose wisely, and you'll have an advocate who supports you every step of the way.

Seller Menu of Services

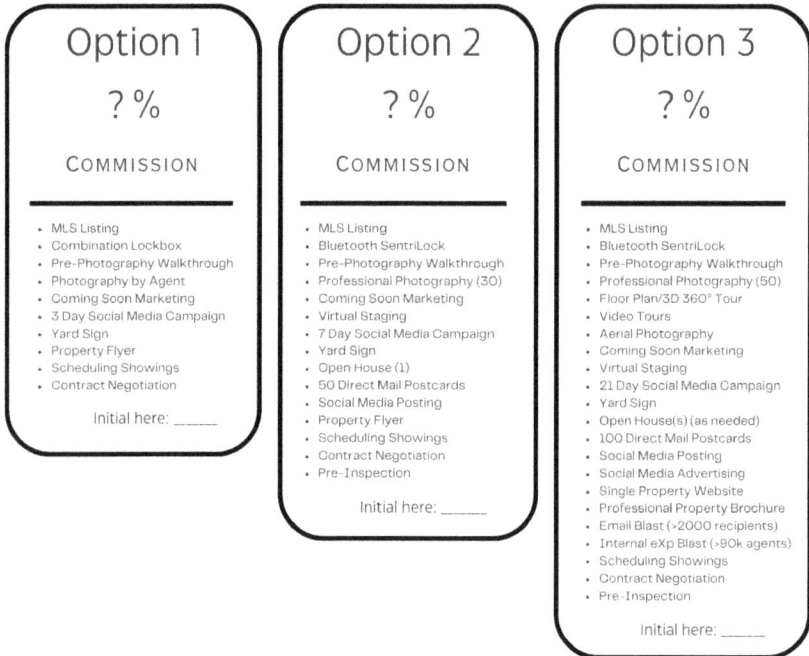

Option 1

? %

COMMISSION

- MLS Listing
- Combination Lockbox
- Pre-Photography Walkthrough
- Photography by Agent
- Coming Soon Marketing
- 3 Day Social Media Campaign
- Yard Sign
- Property Flyer
- Scheduling Showings
- Contract Negotiation

Initial here: _____

Option 2

? %

COMMISSION

- MLS Listing
- Bluetooth SentriLock
- Pre-Photography Walkthrough
- Professional Photography (30)
- Coming Soon Marketing
- Virtual Staging
- 7 Day Social Media Campaign
- Yard Sign
- Open House (1)
- 50 Direct Mail Postcards
- Social Media Posting
- Property Flyer
- Scheduling Showings
- Contract Negotiation
- Pre-Inspection

Initial here: _____

Option 3

? %

COMMISSION

- MLS Listing
- Bluetooth SentriLock
- Pre-Photography Walkthrough
- Professional Photography (50)
- Floor Plan/3D 360° Tour
- Video Tours
- Aerial Photography
- Coming Soon Marketing
- Virtual Staging
- 21 Day Social Media Campaign
- Yard Sign
- Open House(s) (as needed)
- 100 Direct Mail Postcards
- Social Media Posting
- Social Media Advertising
- Single Property Website
- Professional Property Brochure
- Email Blast (>2000 recipients)
- Internal eXp Blast (>90k agents)
- Scheduling Showings
- Contract Negotiation
- Pre-Inspection

Initial here: _____

Figure 6

Post-Sale Considerations:
Moving On and Starting Fresh

Chapter Eleven

The completion of a major sale, whether it's a home, business, or valuable asset, marks the end of one chapter and the beginning of another. This transition period can be both exciting and challenging as it involves significant logistical, financial, and emotional adjustments. This chapter outlines a guide to effectively navigate this process, from managing the practical aspects of moving to planning the next phase of life, ensuring that this fresh start is as smooth and fulfilling as possible.

MANAGING THE LOGISTICS OF MOVING

Moving is one of the most daunting aspects of transitioning post-sale, but with thoughtful planning, it can be transformed into an organized and even enjoyable experience. Here's how to approach it:

Declutter and Simplify
Before packing, take stock of your belongings and identify items that no longer serve you. Selling, donating, or discarding unnecessary items not only lightens the load but also offers a symbolic opportunity to leave behind what no longer fits into your future.

Create a Moving Timeline
Establish a clear schedule, starting from the sale's closing date. Key steps include notifying utility companies, arranging mail forwarding, and hiring movers. If you're relocating to a distant location, account for travel logistics, such as accommodations or transport for pets.

Hire Professionals Where Needed
Whether it's professional movers, storage facilities, or a cleaning service for the property being vacated, outsourcing certain tasks can alleviate stress. Research service providers thoroughly, obtain quotes, and read reviews to ensure reliability.

Pack Strategically

Pack room by room, labeling boxes clearly and creating an inventory. Essentials like toiletries, chargers, and important documents should be kept in an accessible "first-night" box. If storing items temporarily, invest in climate-controlled storage for valuables.

Transition Your Utilities and Services

Make a checklist of all utilities and services to transfer or cancel, including electricity, water, internet, and subscriptions. Notify your bank, healthcare providers, and government agencies of your change in address to avoid disruptions.

Managing Finances Post-Sale

The financial aspect of a sale often comes with complexities, ranging from taxes to reinvestment opportunities. Managing these wisely is crucial for a secure and prosperous future.

Understand Your Tax Obligations

Consult a tax professional to understand any potential tax liabilities stemming from the sale. This might include capital gains taxes, estate taxes, or business-related deductions. Planning for these in advance will help avoid surprises.

Allocate Proceeds Wisely

With the proceeds of the sale in hand, it's time to develop a plan for allocation. Consider the following:

Emergency Fund: Set aside enough for 3–6 months of living expenses.

Debt Repayment: Pay down high-interest debts to improve your financial footing.

Reinvestment: Explore options such as buying a new property, investing in stocks, or starting a new business.

Savings Goals: Allocate funds for retirement, education, or other long-term goals.

Work with a Financial Advisor
A certified financial planner can help you craft a strategy tailored to your needs. They can also advise on balancing short-term liquidity with long-term investment growth, ensuring that your finances remain stable regardless of life's uncertainties.

Budget for Your Next Phase
Develop a detailed budget that reflects your new circumstances. If you're downsizing, your living expenses may decrease, but relocating or renting can introduce additional costs. Account for one-time expenses, such as moving fees, alongside recurring costs like rent or mortgage payments.

Planning for the Next Phase of Life

Starting fresh after a sale presents a unique opportunity to reassess your goals and priorities. Whether you're purchasing a new home, opting to rent, or relocating to a different region, planning intentionally can make this phase fulfilling.

Consider Your Lifestyle Goals
What kind of life do you envision in this next chapter? Whether it's a quiet rural retreat, a bustling urban apartment, or a location closer to family, your decision should reflect your values and aspirations.

Buying a New Home
If purchasing a property is part of your plan, approach the process methodically:

Assess Your Needs: Evaluate factors like space, location, and proximity to amenities.

Secure Financing: Pre-approve a mortgage or determine how much of your sale proceeds you'll use for a down payment.

Partner with a Real Estate Agent: A knowledgeable agent can help you navigate the market and secure a property that aligns with your vision.

Renting as an Interim Solution

Renting can be a strategic choice if you're uncertain about where you'd like to settle. It offers flexibility and time to explore new areas without the commitment of a purchase. When renting, consider the lease terms, monthly costs, and whether the property meets your immediate needs.

Relocating for a Fresh Start

For those relocating to a new city, state, or even country, additional considerations come into play:

Research the Area: Visit potential destinations, explore housing markets, and assess factors like cost of living and local culture.

Network Ahead of Time: Join online communities or reach out to friends and family in the area to build a support network.

Handle Legalities: If relocating internationally, address visa requirements, healthcare coverage, and other regulations well in advance.

Explore Alternative Living Arrangements

In some cases, post-sale transitions may involve alternative living setups, such as co-living, tiny homes, or retirement communities. These can provide opportunities for downsizing, simplifying, or accessing new social networks.

BUILDING A NEW ROUTINE

Establishing stability in your new environment is key to thriving post-sale. Building a routine helps ground you and fosters a sense of control during an uncertain time.

Set Goals for the Future

Whether it's exploring a new hobby, pursuing professional development, or strengthening personal relationships, set concrete goals to focus on.

These aspirations will provide motivation and a sense of purpose.

Create a Home

Turning your new living space into a home involves more than just unpacking. Personalize your surroundings with familiar items, decor, and routines that bring comfort and a sense of belonging.

Engage with Your Community

Building connections in your new environment can enrich your experience. Join local clubs, volunteer, or simply introduce yourself to neighbors to foster a sense of belonging.

Prioritize Self-Care

Transitions can be exhausting, so it's important to prioritize your well-being. Establish healthy habits, such as regular exercise, balanced nutrition, and sufficient rest, to maintain physical and emotional health.

NAVIGATING OPPORTUNITIES FOR GROWTH

A fresh start often brings new opportunities to grow personally and professionally. Take this time to reevaluate what you want to achieve and how to align your actions with your vision.

Professional Opportunities

If you've sold a business, consider whether retirement, consulting, or entrepreneurship is your next step. Explore new industries, attend workshops, or build skills that align with your interests.

Personal Development

The end of one chapter provides space for self-improvement. Whether it's learning a new skill, traveling, or focusing on health, investing in yourself can make the next phase of life deeply rewarding.

CONCLUSION

Moving on and starting fresh after a sale is a multifaceted process that involves careful planning, sound financial management, and a willingness to embrace change. By addressing the logistical, financial, and emotional aspects of this transition, you can turn this chapter into a meaningful opportunity for growth and renewal. Remember, this is not just an ending—it's the beginning of something new and exciting. With thoughtful preparation and a clear vision, you can navigate this journey with confidence and create a future that reflects your aspirations and values.

The Future of the Market: Trends to Watch

Chapter Twelve

As we look ahead, the real estate market continues to evolve, shaped by technological advancements, demographic shifts, economic factors, and environmental concerns. Sellers who stay informed and adaptable will be best positioned to navigate the changing landscape and capitalize on opportunities. This chapter explores emerging trends that will likely influence the future of real estate and offers strategies for staying ahead.

TECHNOLOGY-DRIVEN TRANSFORMATION

The integration of technology into real estate has accelerated, altering how buyers search for homes and how sellers market their properties.

Virtual Reality (VR) and Augmented Reality (AR): These tools allow potential buyers to take immersive virtual tours from anywhere, reducing the need for in-person showings. Sellers who invest in high-quality VR content will have a competitive edge in appealing to tech-savvy buyers.

Artificial Intelligence (AI): AI-powered platforms are revolutionizing how real estate data is analyzed. Predictive analytics can forecast market trends, helping sellers set competitive prices and identify the best times to sell.

Blockchain for Transactions: Blockchain technology is streamlining transactions by enabling smart contracts, reducing fraud risks, and enhancing transparency. Sellers should familiarize themselves with these systems as they become more prevalent.

Takeaway for Sellers

Embrace technology by working with agents or platforms that utilize cutting-edge tools. Invest in professional photography, 3D tours, and

AI-driven insights to attract more buyers.

SUSTAINABLE AND ENERGY-EFFICIENT HOUSING

Environmental concerns are reshaping buyer preferences, with increasing demand for eco-friendly and energy-efficient homes.

Green Certifications: Properties with certifications like LEED or ENERGY STAR are becoming more desirable. Installing solar panels, energy-efficient windows, or smart thermostats can increase a home's appeal and value.

Urban Green Spaces: Urban buyers value proximity to parks and sustainable community designs. Sellers with properties in these areas should highlight such features in their marketing efforts.

Takeaway for Sellers

Consider upgrading your property with sustainable features to align with buyer expectations. Highlight any existing eco-friendly elements when listing your home.

SHIFTS IN DEMOGRAPHICS AND LIFESTYLE PREFERENCES

Demographics significantly influence real estate trends. Understanding the needs of emerging buyer segments is crucial for sellers.

Millennials and Gen Z: These tech-savvy, socially conscious buyers are entering the market in increasing numbers. They prioritize affordability, convenience, and digital amenities.

Aging Baby Boomers: As baby boomers downsize, there's growing demand for smaller, low-maintenance properties. Sellers targeting this demographic should emphasize accessibility features.

Remote Work Revolution: The shift to remote work has changed location preferences. Suburban and rural areas with affordable housing and robust internet infrastructure are experiencing increased demand.

Takeaway for Sellers

Know your audience. Tailor your marketing to the specific demographics likely to be interested in your property, whether it's emphasizing affordability for younger buyers or accessibility for older ones.

Urbanization vs. Suburban and Rural Growth

The pandemic reshaped urbanization trends, with many seeking larger spaces in suburban or rural areas. However, cities remain hubs for culture, jobs, and amenities.

Suburban Growth: Suburban areas are transforming to include urban-style conveniences, attracting a broader range of buyers.

Reurbanization: As cities adapt with better infrastructure and more green spaces, some urban markets are regaining popularity.

Takeaway for Sellers

Monitor local trends to understand where demand is headed. Highlight your property's proximity to desired amenities, whether urban or suburban.

The Impact of Economic Uncertainty

Economic factors like inflation, interest rates, and housing affordability will continue to influence market conditions.

Interest Rates: Rising interest rates can dampen buyer demand, especially for first-time homebuyers. Sellers may need to adjust pricing strategies accordingly.

Affordability Crisis: With housing prices outpacing income growth, many buyers seek creative financing options. Sellers should be prepared to negotiate and offer flexibility.

Global Influences: Economic uncertainty, such as supply chain disruptions or geopolitical tensions, can impact construction costs and market stability.

Takeaway for Sellers

Stay informed about economic indicators. Work with real estate professionals to craft strategies that account for fluctuating market conditions.

REGULATORY CHANGES AND HOUSING POLICIES

Government policies around housing, zoning, and taxes can significantly influence the market.

Affordable Housing Initiatives: Policies promoting affordable housing can affect market dynamics, especially in urban areas.

Zoning Reforms: Changes in zoning laws to allow for multi-use developments can create new selling opportunities.

Tax Incentives: Tax breaks for energy-efficient upgrades or first-time homebuyers can shift demand patterns.

Takeaway for Sellers

Stay updated on local and national policy changes that might impact your property's value or buyer incentives.

PREPARING FOR MARKET VOLATILITY

The real estate market is inherently cyclical. Understanding these cycles and preparing for volatility can help sellers stay resilient.

Local vs. National Trends: Local markets often behave differently from national trends. Sellers should focus on hyper-local data.

Seasonality: Traditional selling seasons may shift due to broader economic and lifestyle changes.

Takeaway for Sellers

Work with agents who have deep knowledge of your local market and can provide real-time insights.

EDUCATION AND ONGOING LEARNING

Staying informed is essential for sellers looking to adapt to future trends.

Market Reports: Regularly review reports from real estate firms, economists, and local boards.

Professional Guidance: Work with real estate professionals who prioritize continuing education and have access to the latest tools.

Community Engagement: Join online forums, attend local events, and network with other property owners to stay abreast of changes.

Takeaway for Sellers

Invest in your knowledge. The better informed you are, the more strategic your decisions will be.

CONCLUSION

The future of real estate promises to be dynamic, with opportunities and challenges shaped by technology, sustainability, economic conditions, and changing buyer preferences. Sellers who stay informed, adapt quickly, and leverage professional insights will remain competitive in this evolving landscape. By anticipating trends and understanding their impact, you can position your property to attract the right buyers and achieve your goals in any market condition.

A Confident Sale Awaits

Conclusion

Selling your home represents more than a mere transaction; it is a significant transition. You have invested countless memories, hard work, and affection into your residence, making the decision to sell a profound one. Nevertheless, with the appropriate information and preparation, this process can be manageable. In reality, it can be a fulfilling experience that offers both financial and emotional benefits as you move forward into your next phase of life.

This book has taken you step-by-step through the complexities of selling a home. From deciding to sell to understanding market trends, each chapter has been designed to equip you with practical tools and insights. Now, as you stand at the threshold of this important decision, it's time to bring it all together. Let's revisit the key themes and why you can approach the sale with unwavering confidence.

KNOWLEDGE IS POWER

The selling journey begins with understanding your "why." In Welcome to the Selling Journey and Deciding to Sell: Is It the Right Time?, we discussed the importance of aligning your decision with your goals. Whether it's upsizing, downsizing, or relocating, clarity about your purpose sets the tone for the entire process. Recognizing market conditions and timing ensures that you approach the sale strategically, not reactively.

Armed with this foundation, you're not just selling a property—you're making an informed, proactive choice. Knowledge eliminates uncertainty, allowing you to anticipate challenges and adapt with ease.

One of the most empowering aspects of selling your home is knowing you've done everything possible to make it shine. In Preparing Your Home for Sale: First Impressions Matter, we highlighted the importance of curb appeal, decluttering, and staging. These efforts not only maximize your home's value but also set a welcoming tone for potential buyers.

By paying attention to details, you send a powerful message: this is a home worth investing in. Buyers can sense care and quality, and these impressions often translate into stronger offers.

THE ART AND SCIENCE OF PRICING

A well-priced home is a magnet for the right buyers. In Pricing Your Home Right: Strategy for Success, we explored the balance between market trends, comparable sales, and buyer psychology. Overpricing can scare off potential buyers, while underpricing risks leaving money on the table.

However, when pricing is approached as both an art and a science, it creates a foundation for a smooth transaction. Trust the data, listen to expert advice, and remember that the goal is to maximize interest while staying competitive.

STANDING OUT IN THE MARKET

In a crowded marketplace, marketing is your chance to differentiate. Marketing Your Home: Attracting the Right Buyers emphasized leveraging both traditional and digital tools to showcase your property's best features. From professional photography to well-crafted listings, these efforts ensure that your home captures attention and generates interest.

Think of your marketing plan as your home's voice, telling its story to buyers. When this story resonates, it creates emotional connections that drive offers.

One of the most pivotal moments in the selling process is when offers start coming in. In Negotiating Offers: Getting the Best Deal, we outlined strategies for evaluating offers beyond the price tag. Terms, contingencies, and timelines all play a role in determining the best fit for your goals.

Negotiation is about collaboration, not confrontation. By remaining firm yet flexible, and always keeping your objectives in mind, you can navigate this stage with poise and professionalism.

SIMPLIFYING THE COMPLEX

The closing process can feel like a whirlwind of paperwork, deadlines, and fine print. In Understanding the Closing Process: From Offer to Sold, we demystified this crucial stage. With a clear timeline and support from your professional team, the steps from accepting an offer to transferring ownership can unfold smoothly.

Remember, you're not in this alone. Your real estate agent, title company, and other professionals are there to guide you. Lean on their expertise to avoid unnecessary stress.

AVOIDING MISSTEPS

Mistakes happen—but they don't have to happen to you. Avoiding Common Pitfalls: Mistakes to Watch Out For highlighted potential challenges, from emotional decision-making to underestimating costs. Being aware of these pitfalls ensures that you approach the sale with eyes wide open.

With preparation, diligence, and patience, even the most common hurdles can be navigated successfully.

Financial Savvy

Understanding the financial implications of your sale is crucial for long-term success. Tax Implications of Selling Your Home and Post-Sale Considerations: Moving On and Starting Fresh provided insight into taxes, reinvestment options, and planning for your future. Selling a home is not just about the immediate gain; it's about setting yourself up for the next phase of life.

Consulting with financial advisors and tax professionals ensures that you maximize benefits and avoid surprises.

The Right Support System

Choosing the right professionals can make all the difference. In Working with a Realtor: How to Choose the Right Professional, we explored the qualities that define a great agent—trustworthiness, expertise, and communication. These professionals act as your advocates, problem-solvers, and negotiators.

Partnering with the right people turns the selling process into a collaborative effort, where your goals are always at the forefront.

Looking Ahead

Finally, in The Future of the Market: Trends to Watch, we looked at the broader real estate landscape. While no one can predict the future, understanding trends gives you the context to make decisions confidently. Markets may fluctuate, but preparation and strategy are timeless.

Walking Away Confidently

As you close this chapter, remember that the selling process is not just about letting go—it's about moving forward. Each step you've taken, from preparation to negotiation, builds toward a successful outcome.

Your home is more than walls and a roof—it's a reflection of your journey, your growth, and your aspirations. Selling it doesn't diminish its value; rather, it passes that value on to someone else while empowering you to embrace new opportunities.

With the right mindset, preparation, and support, you can confidently navigate this process. You're not just selling a property—you're creating a foundation for your next adventure.

So, take a deep breath, trust in the work you've put in, and step forward with confidence. A successful sale awaits—and with it, the promise of a bright and exciting future.

CONGRATULATIONS
YOU HAVE THE TOOLS TO SUCCEED

Navigating the Probate Process for Real Estate

Bonus

The loss of a loved one is a deeply emotional experience, and managing their estate, including any real property, can be overwhelming. This bonus chapter provides a clear overview of the probate process and emphasizes the importance of working with a qualified real estate agent to guide you through this challenging time.

UNDERSTANDING PROBATE AND REAL ESTATE

Probate is the legal process by which a deceased person's estate is administered, including distributing assets according to their will or state laws if no will exists. Real estate, often one of the most significant assets in an estate, requires special attention during probate.

Key steps in the probate process for real estate include:

Validating the Will: If a will exists, the court must validate it to confirm the deceased's intentions.

Appointing an Executor or Administrator: This individual is responsible for managing the estate, including real property.

Determining Ownership: Establish whether the property is held solely by the deceased or in joint tenancy, which can impact probate requirements.

Addressing Debts and Taxes: Outstanding mortgages, liens, or property taxes must be accounted for during the probate process.

THE ESSENTIAL ROLE OF A REAL ESTATE AGENT

Engaging a professional real estate agent early in the probate process can significantly ease the burden on surviving loved ones and ensure the property is managed effectively. A skilled agent provides invaluable expertise and services tailored to both the probate process and any associated estate sale.

Property Evaluation and Preparation
- Conduct a Comparative Market Analysis (CMA) or professional appraisal to determine the property's market value.
- Guide families on preparing the home for sale, including recommendations for repairs, decluttering, or staging to increase its appeal and value.

Marketing Expertise
- Develop a tailored marketing plan using professional photography, online platforms, and targeted advertising to attract the right buyers.
- Collaborate with estate sale organizers to ensure the property is presented optimally, balancing both the sale of personal items and the home itself.

Offer Management and Negotiations
- Handle the review and comparison of offers, ensuring the estate's financial goals are met.
- Negotiate with buyers to achieve the best possible outcome, focusing on maximizing value while addressing time-sensitive concerns.

Logistical Support and Coordination
- Manage property showings, open houses, and communication with potential buyers, ensuring minimal disruption to grieving families.
- Provide a single point of contact for coordinating tasks, especially for out-of-town executors.

The right agent ensures every step—from preparing the property to finalizing the sale—is handled with professionalism and compassion.

For families managing an out-of-state property, working with a local Realtor® is invaluable. Local agents bring:

Market Expertise: In-depth knowledge of neighborhood trends and buyer preferences.

Network Connections: Access to trusted local service providers, from contractors to probate attorneys.

Ease of Communication: Acting as a reliable point of contact for updates, showings, and coordination.

Out-of-town executors benefit from an agent who can handle day-to-day tasks, ensuring the property is well-maintained and marketed effectively without requiring constant travel.

Why My Services Are the Right Fit

As a Realtor® with experience in handling probate-related real estate, I offer:

Compassionate Guidance: I understand the emotional toll of losing a loved one and work with care and sensitivity.

Full-Service Support: From appraisals to closing, I provide end-to-end assistance tailored to your needs.

Local Knowledge: My deep understanding of the market ensures your loved one's property receives maximum exposure and value.

By choosing me, you gain a trusted partner committed to making this challenging journey easier. Let me handle the complexities, so you can focus on what matters most—*honoring your loved one's legacy.*

Dr. Turner has over 30 years of experience as a knowledgeable real estate consultant. His genuine passion for real estate drives him to assist clients and agents in achieving their real estate objectives. He possesses the essential insight and expertise to effectively guide customers, clients, and agents through the complexities of the real estate market. He finds great fulfillment in following the legacy of his late father, Robert L. Turner, who dedicated his life to God, family, and the real estate profession.

Dr. Turner earned his Doctor of Ministry (D.Min) degree in 1999 and subsequently completed a Master of Business Administration (MBA) in 2009. He has been happily married to Minister Lisa Shenee' Phelps Turner for nearly 30 years and takes pride in being the father of four adult children.

In addition to his contribution to real estate, Dr. Turner has devoted three decades to Beulah Baptist Church, serving as its Pastor for 25 of those years. In this capacity, he provides spiritual guidance and support to a committed community of Christian believers.

An accomplished author on various topics, he has also presented his insights and wisdom at numerous professional conferences and has made appearances on national platforms.

Credentials:
- Realtor®
- Seller Representative Specialist
- Military Relocation Professional
- Seniors Real Estate Specialist
- Pricing Strategy Advisor
- Accredited Buyer's Representative
- Certified Relocation Agent
- Certified Express Offers Agent
- Certified VA Loan Agent
- Certified Real Estate Agent Mentor

Marcus E. TURNER
— REAL ESTATE PROFESSIONALS —

**Scan Code for
Assistance, Advice,
and Complimentary Resources**

800 Maine Avenue SW, Suite 200
Washington, DC 20024
202-280-1766 | 833-335-7433 ext. 161
info@marcuseturner.com

www.ingramcontent.com/pod-product-compliance
Lightning Source LLC
Chambersburg PA
CBHW060553100426
42742CB00013B/2545